Freud the Humanist

Charles Rojzman

OPEN GATE PRESS
LONDON

English translation first published in 1999 by Open Gate Press
51 Achilles Road, London NW6 1DZ

Freud: Un humanisme de l'avenir first published in French by
Desclée de Brouwer, 1998

This translation copyright © Open Gate Press
All rights, by all media, reserved.

British Library Cataloguing-in-Publication Programme
A catalogue reference for this book is available from the
British Library.

ISBN: 1 871871 46 8

Quotations from The Standard Edition of the Complete
Psychological Works of Sigmund Freud (Hogarth Press, London,
1953-1974) by permission of A. W. Freud et al by arrangement
with Mark Paterson & Associates

Cover photograph © Freud Museum, 20 Maresfield Gardens,
London NW3 5SX

The quotation from *The Kingdom of this World* by
Alejo Carpentier, in the translation of Harriet de Onís
is © Alfred A. Knopf, Inc, 1957, and included by permission of
A.M. Heath Ltd.

Printed in Great Britain by
The Cromwell Press, Trowbridge, Wiltshire

Charles Rojzman is the founder of *Transformations: Thérapies Sociales*, an institution providing training and advice on how to solve seemingly intractable social problems at home and in the workplace. He is author of several works, including *La Peur, la haine et la démocratie* and *Savoir Vivre Ensemble*, a book about alternative methods of coping with violence and racism. His most recent book is *Comment ne pas devenir electeur du Front National*.

Transformations has recently moved from Paris to Arles, in order to expand its activities.

Contents

Discontent in Civilisation	1
The Childhood of a *Conquistador*	11
A Crazy Undertaking	21
That Primary Hostility 1914-1930	41
The Couch is a Laboratory	59
A Treasure Capable of Enriching our Civilisation	73
Select Bibliography	88

Now he understood that a man never knows for whom he suffers and hopes. He suffers and hopes and toils for people he will never know ... But man's greatness consists in the very fact of wanting to be better than he is ... For this reason, bowed down by suffering and duties, beautiful in the midst of his misery, capable of loving in the face of afflictions and trials, man finds his greatness, his fullest measure, only in the Kingdom of This World.

Alejo Carpentier,
The Kingdom of this World

Discontent in Civilisation

'Thanks to the telescope we can see the stars; we can hear music from New York; we have given marvellous prostheses to our restricted senses. However, why don't we feel good and why do we suffer so many discontents, even more than our ancestors did?' That description of the 'discontent in civilisation' is still true in the time of the Internet and the conquest of Mars. One part of humanity endeavours not to die of hunger, poverty and sickness while the other part, gorged with abundance and consumer goods, forgets its boredom in drug addiction and circus games.

Discontent in civilisation! In some countries, fanaticism and barbarism are offering their own forms of solution to the question of lost meaning, and are threatening to transmit the seeds of fear and hatred to the entire planet. Psychoanalysis attempts to bring a cure to the psychological poverty of the masses which Freud spoke of. But, James Hillman observes, we've had a hundred years of psychotherapy and the world's getting worse. What is there to say? Surely Freud, like others before him, cannot become just a part of the ideal museum of Western man? A piece of culture, one witness among others to the eternal human quest?

No other personality of the contemporary world has been subjected to so much curiosity as Freud, and no other life's work has been subjected to so much study and comment. There are innumerable psychoanalytic practices and scholarly reviews devoted to psychoanalysis in all the cities of the West, and interpretations of a psychoanalytical kind are thriving in magazines. But perhaps this is what is wrong: 'serious' psychoanalysis only addresses its initiates and only convinces those who are already convinced of its validity. Even its language, which is often scholarly, mannered and obscure, distances it from the everyday. For the poor, for the powerless, for the disinherited of the planet, the name of Freud belongs to a culture of wealth which cannot liberate them from poverty and oppression. So is Freud's thought dead, or at the very least useless? What can we hope for from it now that sexual liberation has betrayed its promises and archaic drives are returning almost everywhere, and more than ever, in the world?

For the most part, Freud's research is fundamentally oriented towards infantile sexuality and the treatment of neuroses. Indeed, Freud threw open the locked door of sexuality, stripped the child of its alleged purity and lifted the lid of the witches' cauldron. But Kurt Tucholsky was already writing: 'What is merely fashionable about his writings will pass. The childish joy which Americans and other nations warped by puritanism feel in at last being able to speak publicly of sex is not Freud's fault. The great renewer of old buried truths – of the truth that the man's will is not free – will remain.' And Freud himself was to say, besides: 'The use of analysis for the treatment of the neuroses is only one of its applications; the future will perhaps show that it is not the most important one.'

The most important application of psychoanalysis could well have to do with social pathologies: the rise of fundamentalisms and sectarian phenomena, violence and drug addiction, the passivity of citizens and the corruption of those in power, the sanctification of the Market and of Profit: in short, that human madness which makes communal life impossible or at least difficult ... Goethe said: 'Only that which is fruitful is true.' Far from chapels and idolatrous sects, and without entering into controversies on the limits and errors of the doctrine, let us ask what creates meaning, what is still fruitful in the work of a man who has made his mark on our epoch, whether we like it or not, and who searched honourably all his life for the truth.

The Practice of Doctor Freud: Berggasse 19, Vienna

Psychoanalysis is above all the creation of one man, Sigmund Freud. It was in 1896, about a century ago, that *The Interpretation of Dreams* appeared, the work in which Freud, in accordance with his youthful vows, was to try to 'understand something of the riddles of the world in which we live and perhaps even to contribute something to their solution.' What images do we still have from that time of Freud the man?

The first which imposes itself upon us must be the one of the den where psychoanalysis was forged, the study where he worked. On the desk, a statue of Imhotep, the Egyptian divinity of knowledge and medicine, holds a roll of papyrus on his knees. The ancient statuettes and the oriental rugs which cover the most famous couch fill the famous doctor's study with the perfume of foreign, mystical and mythological pictures and evocations, The warm, exotic and somewhat mysterious atmosphere which holds sway in this study continues to exercise a fascination over biographers and contemporaries. The antique statuettes tell the myths of civilisation and live for the father of psychoanalysis as heralds, across culture, of human desire. Freud holds a dialogue with the past, with the past of humanity just as much as with that of the individual. In this office, psychoanalysis as it is practised and reflected upon, is an archaeological reconstruction of the lost past and a making visible of the eternal laws of the human psyche. The many sick people who crowd into this famous place are surrounded by divinities and sages, and tell of the forgotten emotions, the memories and all the disguises of the soul.

Freud was a simple and rigorous man. His life contained no mysteries, and was not cluttered by complex or legendary events. It was by searching in his soul and through his patients that he discovered the common humanity which suffered, which wept and which hoped. But although he was fascinated by his researches and even though these hours of daily reflection were precious, when he came out of his study, Freud was happy to find his family circle. Moreover, his wife Martha and his children accepted the fact that their father was not very attentive during his working hours because they knew that he was one hundred per cent present during his moments of leisure. Freud dearly loved his family, he liked to take time to walk with 'his little troop', to go gathering mushrooms and strawberries from the woods, or equally to take them to a museum or out fishing.

Freud combined and harmonised his family life and his work in a single place, Berggasse 19. His life was well regulated: after lunch he walked for about an hour in the streets of Vienna, then from three until four in the afternoon he received patients without appointment, then between four o'clock and seven o'clock in the evening – sometimes even later – he devoted himself to his patients whom he saw for forty-five minutes each. Finally, between eleven at night and two in the morning, he set down on paper his ideas, his dreams, his experiences. Large white sheets of paper received the impressions and the analyses left after each interview. Starting from the associations of suffering, of dreams and of childhood, Freud mingled what people had told him with myths and anecdotes. From these, he created the works which left their

It is true that things are moving everywhere, but you seem to overestimate my pleasure in that. What personal pleasure is to be derived from analysis I have obtained during the time when I was alone, and since others have joined me it has given me more pain than pleasure. The way people accept and distort it has not changed the opinion I formed of them when they non-understandingly rejected it. An incurable breach must have come into existence at that time between me and other men.

Letter to Pfister, December 25, 1920

mark on his contemporaries and which have exercised such an influence on our century.

This is the simple yet grandiose picture fixed by posterity and transmitted by the photographs of his adult years and the evidence of his contemporaries. The slightly austere but warm picture of a 'paterfamilias' and a Viennese 'professor' who led a well-ordered bourgeois life; the picture, too, of a scholar and a sage who knew how to see beyond appearances and brought about cures by the magic of his interpretations. Freud did not pay so much attention to this regularity, this simplicity of life which may astonish us. He wrote simply that his external life had passed by calmly and without incident, with only a few dates which should be remembered; and one of his biographers, his friend Stefan Zweig observed: 'Seventy years in the one town and more than forty of them in the same house, carrying on his activities in the same rooms, sitting in the same chair to read or at the same desk to write ... During every week for thousands of weeks he has pursued the same round of circumscribed activities, each day exactly like another. When still attached to the university, he lectured there once a week; on Wednesday evening there was always a gathering of disciples, an intellectual symposium after the Socratic model; on Saturday afternoon, in earlier years, a card party. Apart from these little interruptions, from morning till evening (or rather till long past midnight) every minute was devoted to analyses, the treatment of patients, study, and original writing.'

Freud's real life was that of his soul, in a world where he was both devil and knight, demon and conquistador, a world which was both tortured and serene, the world of an incredible interior research, peopled by monsters, nightmares and illuminating visions. Freud himself did not hide his ambivalence. Although his life was peaceful, and given its rhythm only by births, deaths, studies, work, friendships, it was above all the life of a hero of the intellect. A hero of the intellect, a *conquistador*, as he called himself, who dedicated himself to a grandiose task: the knowledge of the self. Wasn't this the task which the great sages of antiquity considered the ultimate duty?

The Childhood of a *Conquistador*

The great emotions of his life were the same as those experienced by his contemporaries: love, friendship, deaths – and also the tortured history of the century. However, although Freud was hostile to all biography – 'biographical truth is not to be had,' he would say – we know many details of his childhood. Indeed, he would consider it essential to reveal the events and impressions of his childhood, at least those which he considered determining ones. By means of this self-analysis, he would teach us, once and for all, that man's infancy largely determines his destiny.

Sigismund Freud was an inquisitive and open-minded child from his earliest years. It was his life among his family, the context in which he was born, and his origins which were, as the years rolled on, to forge the future dispositions of his mind and, in particular, that curiosity, that rigour, that ambition and that independence of mind of which he was always a living example.

Equally important elements were the 'familial novel' in which he took part, the moves and changes of fortune which the family experienced, the anti-semitism which he experienced more or less directly, and finally the place and time of his birth in the multicultural Austro-Hungary of the 19th century, meeting point of languages, traditions and religions.

'I was born on 6 May 1856 at Freiberg in Moravia, a small town in what is now Czechoslovakia. My parents were Jews, and I have remained a Jew myself.' From his birth the 'familial novel' was already composed and would contribute to deciding his destiny. What does this 'novel' consist of? His mother Amalie, née Nathanson, was a pretty woman twenty years younger than her husband, whose third wife she was. His two brothers – from his father's first marriage – were much older than him. The emotional world of the family therefore presented some complications. But the affection which his mother had for him was absolute. The success and happiness of her son were a priority, and Freud wrote later: 'When you have definitely been your mother's favourite child, you keep for life that feeling of triumph, that sense of confidence in success which almost invariably assures it.'

Jacob Freud, the father who was a textile-merchant in that small town in Moravia, went bankrupt when Freud was three years old, and decided to leave Freiberg to settle in Vienna. But the city offered no other alternative than an even greater precariousness. The family was bordering on poverty but kept its pride. Freud was to keep that almost obsessional concern for earning money and protecting his family from poverty until he was forty years old.

His ambition, the defining trait of his personality, had other causes too, deeper and more secret. Sigismund was seven or eight years old and had just urinated deliberately in his parents' bedroom. Jacob, his father, exclaimed: 'The boy will come to nothing.' Freud was profoundly affected by this experience which he was to tell and analyse himself: 'References to this scene are still constantly recurring in my dreams, and are always linked with an enumeration of my achievements and successes, as though I wanted to say: "You see, I *have* come to something ..".'

But an even stronger determining factor for Freud was the fact of having been born a Jew: 'There was a perception that it was to my Jewish nature alone that I owed two characteristics that had become indispensable to me in the difficult course of my life. Because I was a Jew, I found myself free from many prejudices which restricted others in the use of their intellect; and as a Jew, I was prepared to join the Opposition, and do without agreement with the "compact majority".' He would say even more later: 'I have often felt as though I had inherited all defiance and all the passions with which our ancestors defended their Temple and could gladly sacrifice my life joyfully for one great moment in history.'

Jacob Freud himself was born into a religious environment, yet he did not transmit a true orthodox practice to his children: but a spirit of everyday piety whose torch Freud would carry all his life. 'My father,' he recalled in 1930, 'let me grow up in complete ignorance of everything about Judaism.' So the family were not really practising Jews. But when Sigismund Freud was born in 1856, the Austro-Hungarian empire had only recently stopped persecuting the Jews. And it was not until the decree of 10 July 1866 that they were officially tolerated, and only from that time that their legal emancipation took effect.

That is why, even though Freud never really observed the rites and precepts of his religion, he felt himself to be Jewish. And for Freud, to be Jewish meant above all to be on the fringe, to be a 'nomad of the spirit', to see the world and mankind with a certain perspective, without illusion, without idolatry. Later, he would write that he belonged to a race which in the Middle Ages was held responsible for all epidemics, and which was now being blamed for the disintegration of the Austrian empire and the defeat by the Germans. Such experiences, he observed, have a sobering effect and are not conducive to a belief in illusions.

Even as a child, Sigismund no doubt carried in himself the weight of hostility and hatred. Even the history of his father was a wound. During a walk, his father told him: 'When I was a young man, I went for a walk one Saturday in the streets of your birthplace. I was well dressed, and had a new fur cap on my head. A Christian came up to me and with a single blow knocked off my cap into the mud and shouted: "Jew! Get off the pavement!"' – 'And what did you do?' the child asked. His father's reply was to leave a painful and indelible mark on his son. 'I went into the roadway and picked up my cap.' Freud felt a humiliation and perhaps a degree of contempt for this father

Hannibal had been the favourite hero of my later school days. Like so many boys at that age, I had sympathized in the Punic Wars not with the Romans but with the Carthaginians. And when in the higher classes I began to understand for the first time what it meant to belong to an alien race and anti-Semitic feelings among the other boys warned me that I must take a definite position, the figure of the Semitic general rose still higher in my esteem. To my youthful mind Hannibal and Rome symbolized the conflict between the tenacity of Jewry and the organization of the Catholic church. And the increasing importance of the effects of the anti-Semitic movement upon our emotional life helped to fix the thoughts and feelings of those early days.

The Interpretation of Dreams

who was not strong enough. He would be strong and powerful, and no one would ever make him pick up his hat from the roadway.

The story which his father told him about the hat was intolerable to the child. It seems that from that time, great men, strong and conquering men increasingly became figures of reference to the young Sigismund. Like them, he wanted to become a great man. This is why his favourite hero-figures were Napoleon and Massena – marshals of empire – and also Hannibal and Cromwell ... Conquerors but also rebels against the established order. All these people have certain character traits in common and also the fact that they have started from nothing. Freud always said that his discoveries did not come from his intellectual qualities but from his character, his courage and his honesty. His ambition and his perseverance were born from the admiration of a mother for a favourite child, from the confidence of a father in the gifts of his son, but also from the desire to surpass a father, to show him that one is capable of the greatest things ...

But this admiration for great men was also to have another consequence: from his earliest youth Sigismund would retreat into the world of dreams and imagination. His reading, of vast numbers of books, would give him a definitive taste for the works of thought. This is how it was that, very early in his life, Sigismund became a devotee of literature, history, mythology and religion. His ever-increasing thirst for learning was to lead him to appreciate nothing more than the company of books. The child would be a talented and studious pupil. It is said that he read Shakespeare when eight years old...

Around him, his family was attentive, and his father never ceased to support and encourage the pronounced tastes of his son for books and study. Moreover, much later, for his thirty-fifth birthday, Jacob gave Freud the family Bible in which he wrote in Hebrew: 'My dear son [...] I would say the spirit of God speaketh to you: "Read in My Book; there will be opened to thee sources of knowledge and of the intellect."' Thus his entire life was influenced by the attraction of research and knowledge.

It is not without importance, either, that the child Sigismund passed the essential part of his formative years in Vienna. That city, which at the time was the capital of the huge Austro-

Hungarian empire, attracted vast masses of workers who had come from all the corners of the empire in order to find subsistence in this metropolis whose inhabitants had doubled in number in twenty years. Freud was a youth and a man during the reign of Franz Joseph (1848-1916). This was a period when the town underwent considerable development, both demographic development (900,000 inhabitants in 1869, more than 2,000,000 inhabitants in 1910), and also cultural development, in the sphere of science as well as in literature or music. Moreover, Freud lived for seventy-nine years in Vienna. And it was not an accident that psychoanalysis was born there, because Vienna was a modern city *par excellence*, which experienced an influx of uprooted people. Viennese modernity was, for better or worse, a melting-pot of the new culture. It was from being uprooted, from the weakening of traditional structures, that the minds of this period could pose themselves the new questions of modern societies.

In Vienna, Freud emerged quietly from childhood. Certainly it was difficult to start making one's way in this large town, but Freud, helped by his intellectual capacities, was successful in his secondary educational studies. Sigismund was ambitious. His first interest turned him towards politics, to which he aspired, moved by a sort of curiosity about human affairs. He would say later that he remembered that 'every industrious Jewish schoolboy carried a Cabinet Minister's portfolio in his satchel,' and that an unknown person had prophesied to him one day in the street that he would be a minister. Influenced by one of his friends and with the support of his father, he decided to study law, the antechamber of politics.

But in the end the young Sigismund would opt for science. Why this radical change? It seems that the historical context counts for a lot here: it was in 1863 that Freud enrolled at the university. Four years previously, the publication of Darwin's *The Origin of Species* had had a resounding success: 'The theories of Darwin, which were then of topical interest, strongly attracted me, for they held out hopes of an extraordinary advance in our understanding of the world, and it was hearing Goethe's beautiful essay on Nature read aloud at a popular lecture by Professor Carl Bruhl just before I left school that decided me to become a medical student.'

A Crazy Undertaking

Ambition, perseverance, honesty, rigour and objectivity were Sigismund's essential character traits. The child had now become a man and in 1878, Sigismund became Sigmund Freud. Close to maturity, he embarked upon his long career and would, after years of study and research, satisfy his first aspirations of glory and success. But how and why was psychoanalysis born? What essential things did it contribute to the history of human thought? What explains the expansion and the success which the psychoanalytic movement would experience?

In order to fully understand and grasp the genesis of psychoanalysis we need to go back to Freud's first investigations, to re-experience with him the first years of his studies.

His university career went smoothly and without hindrances, although he was lonely, and in 1881 he obtained his doctorate of medicine. Those years were not particularly striking, but they reinforced the impressions of childhood in his heart. The students who surrounded him were different, richer and a little hostile. At secondary school, and particularly later at university, Freud had, in fact, to experience the anti-semitism which was then beginning to grow in Austria. As he said himself, it was this racial hatred which prevented him from joining the *compact majority* and made him the sort of person who was on the fringe of his age.

That Darwin's fame was at the bottom of his first professional choices is a disquieting matter. When, in 1863, Freud chose science despite his first aspirations, was he guided by an intuition, a happy chance or a series of circumstances? For indeed, he said himself: 'Neither at that time, nor indeed in my later life, did I feel any particular predilection for the career of a doctor. I was moved, rather, by a sort of curiosity, which was, however, directed more towards human concerns than towards natural objects.'

Everything, then, leads us to believe that Freud's ambition, carried along by Darwin's fame, was very strong. But that is not the only reason: the perspective of a scientific vocation was pleasing to Freud because it involved rationality. Experience and practice were important to the young Freud. His thirst for knowledge could not be content with theoretical research, and it was practice and experience which his studies of medicine promised to bring him. His meeting in his first term with Ernst Wilhelm Brücke, his first teacher, started him on a career in the anatomophysiology of the nervous system. Freud was then working on animals; he was not yet dealing with human beings. But a meeting upset everything: his future wife, Martha Bernays; she was twenty-one years old and he already loved her. The prospect of an eventual marriage would oblige him to consider the question of money. He already wanted to have a family and soon thought that he would have to provide for their needs. From that time, his theoretical studies no longer suited him; he had to earn a living. So he abandoned that career, became a doctor of nervous diseases, and became engaged to Martha in June 1882.

This period marks a turning point in Freud's life. He took a new direction. Ambition persisted, but doubt was present. There followed the decisive and important meetings which would propel Freud far from his uncertainties and would lead him on a definitive path, that of curing the human soul.

In March 1896, the word 'psychoanalysis' was used for the first time. It is true that the appearance of the word marks the identification of the discovery, but psychoanalysis, elaborated and built step by step, is not the fruit of an instantaneous discovery. It could only appear and genuinely take on a form after a long gestation which took place inside him and caused him some difficulties. And Freud, the father of this disturbing child, was tested to the full.

In fact, scientific research cannot allow a place to chance. This is why, from the time when he obtained his doctorate of medicine until the creation of psychoanalysis, Freud was to immerse himself into years of apprenticeship, trial and error, experimentation and laborious practice. From 1882, the date which marks the turning of his professional life, Freud would be confronted by all the obstacles, the uncertainties and sometimes, too, the errors which almost always characterise the birth of a great discovery.

The real departure point of Freud's investigations was his arrival at the hospital at Vienna. And it was Ernst Brücke himself, under whose direction he took his first steps towards the heart of science, who advised him, taking account of his financial difficulties, to practise medicine.

Through his experiences with his patients, Freud was finally confronted with the human soul. Practical medicine replaced the laboratory and he took a new direction. But Freud was not enthusiastic and it was even with a feeling of 'death in the soul' that he became a doctor. The prospects of glory perhaps seemed lost to him at that moment. Only the image of the great Charcot, a man whom he would admire and envy, would restore his faith in his future.

Indeed, with Jean-Martin Charcot, Freud experienced a great turning-point in his career. He received a new impetus and discovered hypnosis during his stay in France, first in Paris with Charcot, but also later at Nancy with Bernheim and Liébaut. At that time, hypnosis was the only effective method of treatment for neuroses, especially hysteria. Then, with Breuer, he made a new discovery: the talking cure in which the patient was listened to and told everything which went on in his head, by following associations freely. The method called 'free association' was created.

Although hypnosis was clearly a therapeutic method which offered some results,

Where are you going, Itzig? – I don't know, ask my horse...

> Jewish story told by Freud, 1916-17
> quoted by Marthe Robert,
> in *The Psychoanalytic Revolution*

Freud quickly judged it insufficient. His experience with his first teachers and his first patients forced him to envisage new therapeutic tools. When Breuer put to him his reflections on the case of Anna O., a woman suffering from a serious hysteria, Freud realised that hypnosis, which had allowed Breuer to 'purge' Anna of certain memories within herself, could not really bring about a definitive cure. Freud realised that he had to abandon hypnosis if he wanted to go further and to obtain definite results...

From this point, he served his apprenticeship with his patients themselves. This is why he noted in 1892, in his reflections on Anna O: 'The core of the hysterical attack, in whatever form it may appear, is a memory, the hallucinatory reliving of a scene which is significant for the onset of illness.'

The patients who followed would, as it were, show him and provide him with the appropriate tools. Spontaneously, they asked Freud for an attentive ear, and equally spontaneously they told him their dreams. Freud would draw the essential parts of his discoveries from his consultations. His scientific rigour combined with his open-mindedness would lead him on the one hand never to neglect any of his experiences, and on the other hand not to pass over anything alarming or scandalous which might come to the surface. In this way, and unlike his colleagues or teachers, Freud would work out the role of sexuality in the constitution of neuroses. The conferences which he gave created a scandal, and he had to face detractors and censors who were indignant at the boldness of his suggestions.

However, Freud would leave nothing to chance and his researches – whether they shocked people or not – would analyse all the elements drawn from experience. That is how Freud would find himself confronted with a privileged patient, a patient who was none other than himself. His meeting with Wilhelm Fliess, ear, nose and throat specialist, whom he greatly admired, set this idea in motion. Indeed, in their correspondence Freud was so frank that he called the exchange of letters his 'self-analysis'. And so Freud became his own field of investigation and Fliess was the privileged witness of this. Through his dreams, his memories of childhood and even the emotions he experienced daily while listening to his patients, Freud tirelessly and minutely undertook a task which was really crazy. He would say himself, 'I was set the task of learning from the patient something that I did not know and he did not know himself.'

The great ideas of Freud are generally known: the Oedipus complex and the division of the psyche into three parts: the id, the ego and the superego. It is known that in the view of psychoanalysis, human beings repeat throughout their lives the types of behaviour which were constructed during childhood, and that therapy consists of reliving these past experiences on the analyst's couch. Even though these elements make up an important part of Freud's work, many of them have been subjected to numerous criticisms. What, then, are the genuine insights in Freud's work which can still enlighten us today?

In the first place, Freud shows us that as psychic processes are strictly determined, we are in a position to understand the meaning of psychic manifestations which are habitually considered as fortuitous or without meaning, like dreams, fantasies and slips of the tongue. Thus we may gain a better understanding of the unconscious reasons for certain accidents, illnesses or events which keep recurring in a person's life, and which we used to attribute to destiny or chance.

Since Freud, the idea of repression has acquired its complete meaning. The error and the danger of pre-Freudian psychology was to want to restrain the instincts by means of reason. The instincts do not allow themselves to be restrained, Freud said, and when they are restrained, they never disappear but continue to exist and rise up again in an unhealthy ferment of nervous anxiety-states, troubles of body and mind, illnesses ...

'Forgotten memories were not lost ... but there was some force that prevented them from becoming conscious.'

Freud has also modified our way of looking at the human being by proving, firstly that the past almost entirely determines the present in our psychic life and secondly, that this determination by the past takes place almost entirely without our conscious knowledge. So he has shown us that what lives in our unconscious world acts ceaselessly on our conscious world, generally without our being aware of it, and not always in accordance with our interests.

He has also enabled us to understand that the repression of desires from consciousness does not stop them existing or acting. Thus we can take our most important decisions without being really aware of our genuine motivations. We can also be unhappy or depressed without knowing why. Even more, if our genuine motivations often remain unconscious, it is because we have an interest in not being conscious of them. And this is how the phenomenon of 'resistance' is explained.

Freud has enabled us to understand that a personality is not static but dynamic. Without going into details, we can say, since Freud, that every personality is a seat of conflicts. These conflicts are to do with passions, needs and drives which are the object of repressions, that is to say, rejection from consciousness; there are also reaction-formations, that is to say, apparent attitudes as reaction to a genuine attitude – thus an excessive kindness can be a compensation for a very deep hostility – and finally, there are projections, that is to say, the attribution to others of feelings which one refuses to see in oneself. All these conceptions now make up part of our cultural heritage, even though sometimes in a very banalised form, and they have not outlived their usefulness in helping us to understand human beings in their relations with others.

Freud also allows us to look at the individual in a completely different way. By giving attention to the wounds of infancy, he invites us to feel an absolute respect for this human person who is so fragile and so malleable. Before him, the child was considered as a little adult, or even, in the worst cases, as a little object which could be treated with indifference and malevolence. Even if our modern concern for the child can sometimes seem excessive, it fits well into the grand emancipation movement of the West. The understanding and attention given to the wounds of infancy have invited us to consider madmen, criminals and marginals, too, in a different way, and to regard them as human beings worthy of respect insofar as they are people, even if their behaviour shocks and alarms us. This respect for the human being has transformed our conception of education. Even if we have not yet got everything out of this immense discovery, following the course of a unique individual is an overwhelming and enriching experience.

Finally, the essential thing which Freud has also shown us is that morality in our relations with other, that is to say, courage, honesty, an aptitude to love others, are not virtues of which we should be proud, but the natural consequences of a benevolent destiny. This simple

Long years ago, while I was sitting with a number of other young hospital doctors at our mid-day meal in an inn, a house physician from the midwifery department told us of a comic thing that had happened at the last examination of midwives. A candidate was asked what it meant if meconium (excreta) made its appearance at birth in the water coming away, and she promptly replied: 'it means the child's frightened.' She was laughed at and failed in the examination. But silently I took her side and began to suspect that this poor woman from the humbler classes had laid an unerring finger on an important correlation.

Introductory Lectures on Psychoanalysis

understanding of what makes us heroes or cowards, brutes or refined beings, good or bad, invites us to be indulgent and compassionate.

A certain number of these points of view are much-discussed, but the very discussion and controversy are a clear indicator of their importance: do the experiences of an adult really represent a repetition of the experiences of the child? Are these childhood experiences and the system of inherited behaviour more important than the influence of the environment? Are the decisive experiences of the human being always above all of a sexual nature?

As we have just seen, the tools and base elements of psychoanalysis are manifold. In order to give us the possibility of investigating the unconscious, dreams, slips of the tongue and plays on words, psychoanalysis puts at our disposal not just the tools necessary for a better understanding of ourselves, but also the methodological instruments for a therapy. And so the transference – that is to say, the observation, the understanding and the discussion of the emotional reactions of the patient in his relationship with the therapist – constitutes a privileged means of getting to know his character and consequently his problems. This notion of transference is fundamental: it rests on the idea that we can obtain an understanding of human psychology by revealing the processes which govern human relations.

Once the principal tools of psychoanalysis were forged, the psychoanalytic movement was created very quickly. After the founding in 1902 of the Wednesday Psychological Society, which in 1908 would become the Psychoanalytic Society of Vienna, there followed the creation of specialised journals, conferences and congresses.

Although it is true that the first adepts and practitioners of psychoanalysis were made up only of a restricted circle of Viennese Jewish doctors, success quickly became international. However, even in glory and success, Freud had to continue to face controversies, not to speak of internal schisms in the movement itself, those of Jung and Adler in particular.

Freud's beginnings were really difficult. Psychoanalysis was not easily accepted in the scientific circles of Vienna. At the beginning of the century, Freud felt completely isolated. As he said himself, in Vienna he was avoided and abroad he was unknown. *The Science of Dreams*, a fundamental work published in 1900, was barely mentioned in the psychiatric reviews. People criticised Freud without even having read his books, and criticised his theories because they were shocking. Freud and his adherents were sometimes considered to be sexual perverts, obsessed psychopaths. It was thought that Freudian theories were inciting people to cast off all constraint and to return to a state of licence and primitive savagery, and hence to put civilisation in danger. During a congress of psychiatrists, one participant went so far as to strike the table with his fist when he heard Freud's theories: 'Such a subject does not deserve to be discussed in a scientific assembly; the police are suitable people to concern themselves with it.'

Freud always understood the reasons for this humiliating attitude, which persisted for a very long time in Vienna. 'I treated my discoveries as ordinary contributions to science, and I hoped they would be received in the same spirit. But the silence which my communications met with, the void which formed itself around me, the hints that were conveyed to me, gradually made me realize that assertions on the part played by sex in the aetiology of the neuroses cannot count upon meeting with the same kind of treatment as other communications. I understood that from now onwards, I was one of those who have "disturbed the sleep of the world," as Hebbel says, and that I could not reckon upon objectivity and tolerance ...' He even experienced this hostility as a kind of anti-semitism, a reticence towards Jewish scientists and researchers. So he wrote that he could, with all proper reserve, raise the question of knowing whether the fact that he was Jewish, something he never sought to hide, had not been a contributory factor in the general antipathy towards psychoanalysis.

Freud continued to present his work as a permanent search for the truth. As he said himself: 'Complete theories do not fall ready-made from the sky and you would have even better grounds for suspicion if anyone presented you with a flawless and complete theory at the very beginning of his observations. Such a theory could only be the child of his speculation and could not be the fruit of an unprejudiced examination of the facts.' Freud's originality lay in this, a theory – indeed a philosophy – based on the results of practice. He said on many occasions: how could his adversaries not see what his discoveries had cost him in slow, patient work?!...

Freud considered that he had invented

nothing and that he was nothing other than an adventurer. So he was happy to regard himself as a 'conquistador'. As he said to Marie Bonaparte on 7 October 1925: 'No, it is not [that I] am modest [...] I have a high opinion of what I have discovered, but not of myself. Great discoverers are not necessarily great men. Who changed the world more than Christopher Columbus? What was he? An adventurer.'

Today, it is difficult to imagine how much Freud's first discoveries must have shocked his colleagues in medicine and at the university. He had to follow the path on which his intuition – and also his unbiased observation of reality – had set him, and it was radically *other*: for psychology in his time, the instincts had to be – and could be – restrained by the reason of civilised and cultivated man. This social ethic corresponded with the illusions of a time which believed in the progress of science and technology and which considered its morality as indisputable and universal. By proving that restrained instincts never disappeared, and that on the contrary, when repressed in the unconscious, they came back with even greater force and noxiousness to disturb physical and mental equilibrium, Freud dealt a cruel refutation to these illusions. Far from wanting to reawaken man's savagery, he claimed that becoming conscious of what was sleeping dangerously in the bottom of people's souls could help intelligence and reason to discipline the instincts.

This discovery of Freud's has certainly profoundly changed our conceptions of the life of the soul, but above all it points the way to a therapy. Some years later, Melanie Klein, one of Freud's disciples, observed that if the attempts to improve humanity, and particularly to make it more peaceful, had failed, this was because no one had ever understood the profundity and the power of the aggressive drives innate in each individual. What these reformers of humanity were trying to do was essentially to encourage the positive, benevolent tendencies of each man, while denying or suppressing his aggressive tendencies. And consequently, from the beginning, their efforts were doomed to failure. Psychoanalysis, Melanie Klein thought, had other methods at its disposal for a task of this sort. She believed that it certainly could not make the aggressive drives disappear completely. But, by reducing the anxiety which strengthens these drives, it could break the alternating game constantly engaged in by hatred and fear.

That Primary Hostility 1914-1930

From 1914, after the assassination at Sarajevo, Freud was faced, like all his contemporaries, by the anxieties, apprehensions and confusions which came with the break-out of the first world war. As he died in 1939, he did not have to live through the appalling second war, but the experience of the first would be enough to throw his researches into complete question. Freud's theories about the human psyche which were formulated before the war would, in fact, seem to him totally incomplete in the light of its hatred and fanaticisms. So he would come to envisage a death instinct, and to introduce new concepts.

In 1914 he was faced with serious financial difficulties and, like many of his contemporaries, he was to see his sons leaving for the front, The period which followed, until the end of the war, was no more fruitful for his researches, either, and Freud was relatively unproductive. However, during these four years, he persevered with certain questionings which would allow him, later, to enrich his work with new hypotheses. It was precisely because the war was not just world-wide, but also – and particularly – barbaric, that the man who had set himself the task of understanding the ways in which the human psyche functioned could not fail to question himself and to look for the causes of such a chaos.

So Freud's life was profoundly disturbed by the war and by the questionings which it aroused. The first world war, the Great War, was, curiously, at first a source of nationalistic enthusiasm for him. But he very quickly became disenchanted and grasped the absolute horror of this war in which the European nations were tearing themselves apart. And it was precisely as a consequence of this war, and of the horrors that accompanied it, that he came to understand for the first time that barbarism can overwhelm civilisation, that no civilisation is safe from these archaic collective drives, and that the death instinct of which he would have to speak later is always present, lurking in the shadow. It was this shadow which henceforth Freud would spend his whole life tracking down in order to try and discover all its secrets. It was this shadow that was the object of his work, the shadow which is also present in each one of us and which he recognised first in his own dreams.

In 1918 the war ended and the world finally made a genuine entry into the twentieth century. Freud wrote to Ferenczi: 'It is a good thing that the old should die, but the new is not yet there.' This new world is the one in which we are living, in the age of uncertainty and questionings about our survival. The two world wars and the innumerable ones which have followed have shown us that we can no longer believe in an unlimited progress marked by the triumph of reason.

Freud was sixty-two when the first war ended and, even though he had been scarred by it, it was clear that the greatest sufferings were yet to come. And indeed, the time after the Great War would be much harder still for him. Inflation ruined him completely and he would be confronted head on by death and illness. From this time his researches would be profoundly influenced and haunted by the idea of death and destruction.

The aftermath of war was firmly marked by personal dramas. Freud lost his daughter Sophie in 1920, and also his grandson Heinz,

Sophie's son, in 1923. He was also confronted with his own physical decline: in 1917 a cancerous tumour was detected in his jaw. But Freud refused to weaken, and continued to work despite everything.

It is this constant work based on experience which explains the very evolutionary character of Freud's work. He added to, revised and completed his work as his life, his history and his thought evolved. And so we may observe that before he was confronted by death and war, by hatred and sickness, Freud was thinking of gathering all the drives under the category of the libido and of self-interest. Then he discovered that he could not be satisfied with the hypothesis that there was a life-instinct. Observation bore its fruits and Freud came to envisage, in opposition to the life-instincts, the existence of death-instincts which were turned against oneself, and of instincts of destruction which were turned against the external world. And so, between 1919 and 1920, he wrote *Beyond the Pleasure Principle*, where he establishes the hypothesis of a death-instinct, a 'Thanatos' as he would call it later, which could be opposed to 'Eros'.

But, as usual, Freud was not content just to propose new concepts, but analysed them each time in great depth so that he might, eventually, draw from them instruments of cure: 'The existence of this inclination to aggression, which we can detect in ourselves and justly assume to be present in others, is the factor which disturbs our relations with our neighbour, and which forces civilisation into such a high expenditure of energy.' And more gravely still: 'The fateful question for the human species seems to be to be whether and to what extent their cultural development will succeed in mastering the disturbance of their communal life by the human instinct of aggression and self-destruction.'

Thus it was that, in 1920, Freud asked himself about the deep causes of the violence exercised by the State or by certain social groups; violence which was accepted passively, and sometimes even enthusiastically, by the masses. Just like the thinkers of the eighteenth century in the days of the Enlightenment, he wanted to struggle against collective irrationality, against the infantile attitudes of submission and the explosions of violence which provoked a regression in civilisation, rights and individual liberties.

Freud's preoccupations in these difficult times show very clearly and in a definitive

But if this one hope [of universal love] cannot be at least partly realised, if in the course of evolution, we don't learn to divert our instincts from destroying our own kind, if we continue to hate one another for minor differences and kill each other for petty gain, if we go on exploiting the great progress made in control of natural resources for our mutual destruction, what kind of future lies in store for us?

To Romain Rolland, 4th March 1923

manner that his real quest, like that of sages of all times, was the 'salvation of man'. And for him, this 'salvation' consisted in attaining knowledge of the truth, the only light which man has at his disposal to guide himself on this earth. But Freud would never cease to say that for this, man must become conscious of the mysterious forces which live within him, in order to be able to control them and govern them. In this matter, he is indeed the heir of Goethe, Spinoza and the philosophers of the Enlightenment.

Moreover, if Freud took up the dominant thought of the Enlightenment, it was because the errors of the twentieth century encouraged old battles to return. When the thinkers of the eighteenth century denounced the oppression of society by the nobility, the wealthy bourgeoisie and the financiers, what they had to say is just as relevant to our so-called democratic societies. Dominant powers and hierarchies still exist, and beneath the appearances of an organised society there exists a state of generalised war, as Rousseau said. Violence has simply taken on more subtle forms, ruled by institutional and apparently consensual norms. The passion for control is always present. Rooted in men's hearts, it reveals itself in the envy and jealousy which constantly destroy social bonds.

One consequence of the war was that all who had put their hopes in the triumph of right and reason – Freud among them – were left distraught and profoundly disappointed. Barbarism continued to be present and, from 1918 until 1939, men of the time were aware, rather as we are today, that collective archaic drives were returning and would take centre stage. This is why it was inevitable that Freud's preoccupations would turn towards cultural questions, questions of civilisation, and especially violence, which seemed to him always to have characterised men's relationships with one another.

So Freud became aware in 1920 that there are death drives in us which we can neither ignore nor ever totally rid ourselves of. Consequently he deduced that if we think that reason is a psychic force capable of containing and governing our drives, we are deluding ourselves. The essential thing for him then became to destroy and to unmask our great illusions and to work to find other ways of fighting against the phenomena of domination, fanaticism and intolerance.

This new interest clearly dates from the First World War which had seen the collapse of European illusions and of the belief in unlimited progress marked by the triumph of reason and universal peace. At the beginning of the twentieth century, scientists and philosophers had still believed that humanity would be capable of overcoming the absurdities of wars and tyrannies. By force of will. By force of consciousness.

From a certain moment, then, Freud, who dreamed in his youth that he would be a political and social reformer, and who referred to himself later as a conquistador, turned his back on individual psychology in order to concern himself with psychology of religions and mass psychology. He wrote to one of his friends about this new concern, saying that he had only wanted a little affair, and that here he was, at his age, forced to marry a new wife.

Then the writings which clearly reveal Freud's concern for the ills and shortcomings of our societies began to appear. *The Future of an Illusion* in 1927 and *Civilization and its Discontents* in 1929. During his more sombre years, Freud worked the fastest, as if, perhaps, the ghosts of the war and of his approaching death were impelling him to complete his work. In fact, illness gnawed at him ever more, and after his first operation in April 1923, he would undergo some thirty surgical operations. He was also obliged to wear a prosthesis in his jaw, which he would call – with some irony but no doubt also much bitterness – 'his monster'. Then there was the great and grievous experience of the death of his mother Amalie, and this at the moment when he was so physically ill. We are in 1930, and Freud has just received the Goethe prize.

During this period, Freud met men, thinkers who, like him, were struggling to find ways of preventing the processes of war. His friends at that time, with whom he met or corresponded, were no longer only doctors; he mixed with writers like Romain Rolland and also with researchers attached to other disciplines than his own. All of them had in common this desire to check hatred and violence. Einstein was among those who saw in Freud a new man, a Freud who was profoundly concerned to resolve the problems of the world. It was essentially with war in mind that the two men would meet. This is what he wrote to Freud: 'I admire the passion which drives you constantly to look for the truth, a passion which seems gradually to have supplanted all the others in your thinking. You show, with an amazing lucidity, the point to which the instincts of aggression and destruction form an integral part of the human soul, alongside those other instincts, love and the desire for life. I think I understand also that you are completely attached to this immense task of liberating man from the ills which war inflicts on him, whether this is from without or even in his mind. This has always been the wish of the greatest intellectual guides of all times...'

So, as in his youth, Freud's real need was 'understand something of the riddles of the world in which we live and perhaps even to contribute something to their solution.' It was no longer a question of being a doctor to a few sick people, but – if possible – of saving humanity from the ills which threatened to destroy it.

Freud took up the endeavour of the Enlightenment to struggle against the different forms of oppression, fanaticism and intolerance, but he added these question which are of such great importance today: 'what allows us to explain the hold which irrational beliefs have over men? What allows us to understand that the evidence of reason can be brutally replaced by expressions of an individual and collective madness?'

The deepest and most relevant analysis which he made then concerned the phenomenon of illusion and as a consequence, that of religion. What Freud wanted to bring to light was that in religion there persists a fundamental structure of illusion, and that this structure is defined by the capacity to awaken or to reawaken infantilism by opposing reason and the spirit of reality. When he spoke of religion, Freud described an hallucination which deceived men about themselves and about the reality which surrounded them, an hallucination which, most of the time, ensured its domination by means of violence, tyranny and destruction. Freud sought to demonstrate this lesson, which has clearly not been properly learned, which history has brought to us through the horrors committed in the name of religion, or of any other ideology of religious tenor, that spirit which we find in the Inquisition, in persecutions, and in fratricidal wars in the name of a god who is claimed to be the true god.

Here we see Freud's project, to bring illusions out into the light of day, and to cure man by letting his autonomy conquer. Man can arrive at this point by becoming aware of his unconscious motives, but also by using this awareness to develop his critical consciousness. It is a question of building a life without illusion and without falsehood. But the task is not a simple one.

Although Freud at first showed himself to be close to the spirit of the Enlightenment, he was nonetheless quite distinctly differentiated from it. The difference between Freud and the thought of the Enlightenment philosophers, with the exception of Rousseau, was that Freud – precisely because he lived in the twentieth century – lost all illusions in a progress led by science and reason. As we have already seen, he lost their optimism and he no longer believed in the powers of reason:

'Have you learned nothing from history? Once before an attempt of this kind was made to substitute reason for religion, officially and in the grand manner. Surely you remember the French Revolution and Robespierre? And you must also remember how short-lived and miserably ineffectual the experiment was. The same experiment is being repeated in Russia

The communists believe that they have found the path to deliverance from our evils. According to them, man is wholly good and is well disposed to his neighbour; but the institution of private property has corrupted his nature. [...] If private property were abolished, all wealth held in common, and everyone allowed to share in the enjoyment of it, ill-will and hostility would disappear among men. [...] I have no concern with any economic criticisms of the communist system; I cannot enquire into whether the abolition of private property is expedient or advantageous. But I am able to recognise that the psychological premisses on which the system is based are an untenable illusion.

                              Civilisation and its Discontents

at the present time, and we need not feel curious as to its outcome.' So Freud no longer believed that an enlightened judgement was sufficient to liberate men, and he no longer believed that the struggle against despotism and the authoritarian installation of an egalitarian and fraternal society was sufficient to change human nature. And so he called the rationalist optimism of the Enlightenment into question, because he knew that human beings never know themselves fully because of their capacities for illusion about themselves.

More still, Freud's analyses allowed him to understand that even ideal collectives centred around notions of progress, science and reason contained their share of illusion, just as much as the religious dogmas and the manifestations of political and social unreason which the thinkers of the Enlightenment denounced. More still, for him, these ideal collectives could contribute to reproducing a form of tyranny. He thought that our societies, which have replaced religious dogmas with new myths deriving from a superstitious belief in progress and science, had invented new forms of oppression. This is why it was not sufficient to attack oppressive institutions and powers, but was also necessary to understand the passionate dimension of individuals, their tendencies to domination and their consent to subjection. Freud proved that illusions remained present, even when erroneous beliefs had been dissipated by the progress of science, because they were constantly being born from archaic desires and conflicts. Illusion – including rationalist illusion – is born from the need to be protected while being loved. According to Freud, this is the function of religion; but when religion loses its hold, man looks for substitutes in ideologies or even narcotics, which allow him to forget the threats of reality and internal conflicts. The modern ascendency of sects and ideologies, the growth of drug-addiction and the use of tranquillisers in today's world, are proof that the magic need for protection is more present than ever.

So what Freud criticised in religion was not the myths or the beliefs, but a fundamental structure of illusion whose presence he noted just as much in other ideologies which claimed to be free of gods. And he showed that it is this capacity of illusion which, by means of a phenomenon of regression, brings infantile factors to the surface, organises them in opposition to reality and reason, and ends by giving human desire nothing but deceptions and hallucinations which, in their turn, create violence and destruction. In this way Freud makes us think, and observe that twentieth-century Western man, who appears to have freed himself from his myths and his gods, is no more free from internal demons and psychic conflicts.

So, whether it is a question of religion, of a party, of a clan or of what we now call 'a unique thought', it seems that the fundamental structure always remains much the same. For Freud, it was clear that 'if you want to expel religion from our European civilisation, you can only do it by means of another system of doctrine, and such a system would, from the outset, take over all the psychological characteristics of religion – the same sanctity, rigidity and intolerance, the same prohibition of thought – for its own defence.'

The Couch is a Laboratory
1930-1939

In 1932 Freud wrote *Why War?* He was seventy-six years old and knew that he was near his end. For him, it was time to hope that the work which he had embarked upon would soon be continued. He still wrote, corresponded with his friends and pursued his research. But unfortunately, all too soon, he would watch the rise of Nazism in pain and physical suffering. And so, having already lived through the first war, illness and also bereavements, Freud would have to face an intensification of anti-semitism and also – and especially – exile. What exactly would he draw from these painful experiences?

When Freud wrote *Why War?* he knew the elements which made up hatred, domination and war. He already had a premonition of how important the social pathologies were, and he believed that psychoanalysis had something to say about the interpretation of cultural phenomena. Once again, he started from a reflection upon religions to demonstrate that all too often men traded their personal neurosis for a large collective neurosis: 'The analogy between religion and obsessional neurosis can be followed out [in ... great detail], and ... many of the particularities and the vicissitudes in the formation of religion can be understood in that light. And it tallies well with this that devout believers are safeguarded in a high degree against the risk of certain neurotic illnesses; their acceptance of the universal neurosis spares them the task of constructing a personal one.'

But these collective neuroses, with their moments of madness, prevent men from living in peace with their fellows. And, as Stefan Zweig writes in his book about Freud: 'The fine art of mutual understanding so essential to satisfactory human relationships and ever more needed as between nations [is] the only art that can help us in the upbuilding of a higher humanity.'

So the big question which presents itself is whether this madness is innate, whether it is part of human nature, or whether it is induced by social hierarchies, by arbitrary institutions founded on violence, which hide the fact that laws are made for the benefit of those who are dominant. Violence in the form of a desire

Fundamentally, indeed, every religion is ... a religion of love for all those whom it embraces; while cruelty and intolerance towards those who do not belong to it are natural to every religion ... If today that intolerance no longer shows itself so violent and cruel as in former centuries, we can scarcely conclude that there has been a softening in human manners. The cause is rather to be found in the undeniable weakening of religious feelings and the libidinal ties which depend upon them.

Group Psychology and the Analysis of the Ego

to dominate and to destroy the other is always latent in our societies. Those who are dominated accept it because they have found ways of dominating in their turn or because they have hope of so doing. Hatred and mistrust of the other are always present. So must we transform social relationships and political power? Must we believe – as Freud put it – that 'the inclination to aggression is an original self-subsisting instinctual disposition in man'? For him, in fact, this presence in man of innate aggression, sadism and masochism was proof that there is a core of madness and insane megalomania in humanity.

It is true that Freud believed that people desired the happiness of sociability, but he sought to show that there also existed a tendency to aim for a megalomaniac happiness, demanding satisfaction for the passions without any brake, and being unaware of their harmful effects on others and on the community. Freud believed that man was always tempted to abuse power. The philosophers of the Enlightenment thought that it was necessary to balance our unlimited desires for pleasure and domination with the force of a social equilibrium based on contracts and laws.

So a determining influence was accorded to education. Freud thought this idea valuable, but added a supplementary element of analysis: he showed that first of all it was necessary to have a clear understanding of the tension between the irrationality of the passions and any adaptation to social equilibrium, and secondly that it was necessary to define how it was that megalomaniac happiness which could give the enjoyment of power entailed an insensitivity to others. This is why the tyrant and the despot lose contact with the reality of others and shut themselves up into the madness of desires without limit. We might add that these insanities which were once the sole preserve of a minority of powerful men seem today, in our mass civilisations, to be very widespread.

For Freud, then, it was not just oppression by a political power which was the origin of attitudes of submission and domination, but rather universal propensities which are a constitutive part of man; propensities which civilisation has not really succeeded in rooting out. Freud was one of the first to reveal that the fact that illusions persist in our world – even though it appears to be dominated by scientific progress and the triumph of reason – shows the ever-present possibility of regression to infantile attitudes. In this crisis of civilisation – which is still with us, and which re-awakens the psychic conflicts bound to infantilism – Freud's desire was to struggle against the threats of internal chaos which create destructive drives. He thought that only an elite of men capable of ruling their lives and their thoughts according to the rationality contained in humanistic values could help civilisation to exercise some control over these regressive phenomena. He suggested in a letter to Einstein that 'a ... stratum of men' should be educated 'with independent minds, not open to intimidation and eager in the pursuit of truth, whose business it would be to give direction to the dependent masses.' These men would have subordinated their emotional life to reason and would constitute a sort of counterweight with the aim of neutralising intolerance and violence. 'Our best hope for the future is that intellect – the scientific spirit, reason – may in the process of time establish a dictatorship in the mental life of man. The nature of reason is a guarantee that afterward it will not fail to give man's emotional impulses and what is determined by them the position they deserve.'

But Freud himself was sceptical about whether it was possible to form an elite liberated from their drives who would know how to compel the world to control its violence. After all, what could be done with the internal chaos which all those who were not part of this elite would have to manage?

Until now, all attempts to bring the feeling of internal chaos under control have failed, and this clearly indicates where the real work of education needs to begin, as Freud wished. The remedies which men in society think they have found to save them suffering from this feeling actually strengthen and reinforce the phenomena of hatred, violence and illusion. We can see this happening today in our society, where human beings threatened by this feeling of internal chaos – which itself is powerfully reinforced by social conditions – are turning to group narcissism and nationalism in search of that narcissistic reassurance, that feeling of all-powerfulness which seeks an object to destroy. This feeling of internal chaos is accentuated today because the models of value and prohibition are either diffuse or are in conflict, and so can no longer be regarded as representatives of a coherent and rational community. As Wilhelm Reich has shown, the coherence which previously governed our lives was a false coherence resulting from an adaptation to a social reality which could be called sick because it hindered creativity and vitality. What is collapsing today is that false, seemingly rational coherence which had a neurotic Superego as its foundation. It is a fact that indispensable forms of security are disappearing in this collapse, a security which men will find again by joining together with those of their immediate group and by expressing intolerance and destruction towards others. Freud considered that it was the forces of Eros which united men in communities but that at the same time, these links, which the fragility of individuals rendered indispensable, excluded those who belonged to other groups. In *Civilization and its Discontents* he wrote: 'When the apostle Paul had posited universal love between men as the foundation of his Christian community, extreme intolerance on the part of Christendom towards those who remained outside it became the inevitable consequence.'

So feelings of hatred towards strangers are an expression of pathological forms of narcissism. And this narcissism is regressive in the same degree as it is collective. Freud saw clearly that conflicts between social reality and the individual could be greatly lessened when there were close identifications between the individual and the community. But he also showed that they could be at the origin of a process of alienation and a threat to individual identity. Thanks to this identification, the group narcissism which is so prevalent today in different countries – whether it takes the form of nationalism, of ethnic group or others – brings love, security and a feeling of worth; but at the same time, it is immensely destructive of individuals' autonomy and of their capacity for objectivation and reality-sense.

In excavating the three-fold nature of the world's soul, Freud brought up something indescribable, words which disturbed; he showed men what they were, with their limits, their errors and their horrors. He said one day that he had made man undergo his third narcissistic humiliation. The first was brought about by Copernicus, who had destroyed the belief that the world was at the centre of the universe;

It is always possible to bind together a considerable number of people in love, so long as there are other people left over to receive the manifestations of their aggressiveness.

Civilization and its Discontents

the second by Darwin, who had shown that man did not occupy a unique place in the scale of creatures; and the third, finally, was the one for which Freud was responsible, by depriving man of the pride he took in his rationality and putting him face to face with the seemingly unfathomable chasm of his unconscious. *Homo sapiens* certainly, and capable of the highest realisations of thought and technology, master of the world; but also *Homo demens*, mad man, sick animal, eternal child, capable of every cruelty and of the most horrendous massacres.

Classical psychiatry drew a clear distinction between the normal man and the mad man, the victim of his insanities. Freud taught us that normal man is not far from the psychotic and that his dreams bear witness to this. Henceforth, every civilisation would need to take account of the existence of these aggressive drives and to realise that it was not just mortal, as Paul Valéry said, but also mad and sick. Henceforth, every man would need to know that he had a monster inside him and that he had to learn to get to know it and to tame it; that for fear of projecting this monster on others, he needed to eliminate it from the surface of the world in order finally to know a reign of justice and happiness.

If we start from here, the genuine meaning of Freud's work wells up more clearly again: it is a question of getting to know the profound characteristics of *Homo demens* who is a part of us and whose existence we must accept, and of being able to envisage the construction of a society which would favour and genuinely encourage the blossoming of our propensities for sociability, love and tolerance.

In 1933, Freud heard that his books had been burned in Germany. It was the return of the great autodafés. 'The world is transformed into an enormous prison. Germany is the worst of its cells.' On 11th March 1938, the Nazis seized power in Austria, and on 22nd March, Freud observed simply of his daughter, 'Anna to the Gestapo.' The danger now seemed imminent in Austria, but Freud still did not want to leave Vienna. He had to wait until Marie Bonaparte and Ernest Jones arrived to convince him before he would go into exile in England. And Franklin Roosevelt himself, the President of the USA, intervened personally so that he should be well treated. And so, on 4th June 1938, Freud finally left with Martha and Anna. It was goodbye to Vienna, the city in which he had passed seventy-nine years of his life.

After arriving in London, Freud was threatened only by illness. He lived in peace, received many visitors and continued to work. And even while receiving many personalities like Stefan Zweig or Salvador Dali, he finished his *Moses and Monotheism*. But on 16th June 1939, affected by a gangrene which was working its way into his jaw, he asked his doctor to make an end of it. On 21st September, two thousand milligrammes of morphine put him into a coma. And so Freud died on 23rd September 1939.

A Treasure Capable of Enriching our Civilisation

Freud died late enough to see his books publicly burned under the Nazis, but too soon to see with his own eyes that barbarism is always present in the heart of our civilisation. But how could Freud even have begun to imagine what would happen? Nonetheless, on this matter, he said to his disciple Jones about the auto-dafés of 1933: 'What progress we are making. In the middle ages they would have burnt me; nowadays they are content with burning my books.' How could he ever have imagined that ten years later his six sisters would die, burned in the gas chambers of a concentration camp? Even so, in 1937, he wrote, with a certain pessimism, that there was no way of checking the Nazi invasion and its cortège of unhappiness for psychoanalysis, as for everything else; and that his only hope was that he would not live long enough to see it.

Adorno said that the goal of all education was to prevent Auschwitz. Freud, who did not live long enough to know of the existence of concentration camps, had nonetheless understood this when he proposed to make man conscious of his mad side and to help him, even if only a little, to be less its victim.

The whole of Freud's work in fact consisted of recognising that barbarism was present in civilisation; that the most murderous instincts were part of man, and that civilisation was simultaneously something which harmed man in his quest for pleasure and a construction always to be begun again.

The greatness of Freud's work is precisely the dialogue with the murderous past of the race, which the varnish of civilisation makes us forget, but which the furies and horrors of war recall to our minds. It is also the dialogue with the evil which we force ourselves so hard to hide, even to the point of expelling it from us in the form of the devil and his accomplices, and of all the figures of the disturbing enemy who is always ready to destroy us. This familiarity with evil was always hurled at Freud in reproach. It was in the name of the 'nobility of the soul' that the Nazis burned Freud's books. It is still in the name of this nobility of the soul that the worst persecutions are committed. Perhaps – this is a bold hypothesis, it must be admitted – Freud the Jew was searching to protect himself in advance from anti-semitism by inventing a way of reconciling man with his accursed part in order, finally, to find the peace which reconciles the world of the instincts and darkness with the sunlight of reason.

Freud's real quest was, by exploring the power of hatred, to discover the genuine bond of love which could unite men. He recognised that these bonds of love existed anyway, that in identifying with a leader, men recognise each other as brothers, but that as they do not recognise their secret desire – acted out in the origins of humanity – to kill the father whom they both adore and hate, they are obliged to kill those outside themselves who represent the rebellious sons. So how can we liberate ourselves from the war which is always present in the history of civilisations, and which continues to be a threat in this twentieth century which has invented the most terrifying weapons of destruction?...

Freud put it clearly: his psychoanalysis, patiently built out of his experience as a doctor of souls, is not complete. What he was seeking, the goal which he wanted to attain, is still far

I had to open for myself a way on my own, and step by step through a tangled jungle. It is not surprising that my path is not very wide and that I have not been able to go very far.

Quoted by Ernest Jones,
The Life and Work of Sigmund Freud

off. Once again, it is not a question of curing a few sick people, but of the health of humanity itself. Freud thought that his first investigations, his first discoveries – important though they were – only indicated a direction. Towards the end of his life he thought of himself like Moses on the threshold of the Promised Land. The prophet would never see this land for which he had so hoped, but he had led his people as far as he could, the furthest possible, with honesty and determination. 'Do you know that I am the Devil?' Freud said one day. 'All my life I have played the role of the Devil so that others might build the most beautiful cathedrals with the materials I have brought them.'

Seen in this light, Freud's couch was the laboratory for a revolutionary experiment which is real 'social dynamite'. And although little that is accurate has been said about it, although Freud's message has been misrepresented, although Freud has been betrayed by his 'slave-sons', to use Jung's expression, it was because that message was still too radical for his epoch and because people only heard one part of it, the part which dealt with sexuality and infancy. His message has been 'medicalised', as if it was simply a question for him of reducing eccentricities or marginalities, of helping suffering beings to adapt to the society of the time.

'Under the influence of this war,' he was already writing to one of his correspondents in 1914, 'I venture to remind you of two assertions psychoanalysis has put forward which have assuredly contributed to its unpopularity.

'Psychoanalysis has concluded from a study of the dreams and mental slips of normal people, as well as from the symptoms of neurotics, that the primitive, savage and evil impulses of mankind have not vanished in any individual, but continue their existence, although in a repressed state – in the unconscious, as we call it in our language – and that they wait for opportunities to display their activity.

'It has furthermore taught us that our intellect is a feeble and dependent thing, a plaything and tool of our impulses and emotions; that all of us are forced to behave cleverly or stupidly according as our attitudes and inner resistances ordain.

'And now just look at what is happening in this wartime, at the cruelties and injustices for which the most civilised nations are responsible, at the different ways in which they judge of their own lies, their own wrong-doings, and those of their enemies, at the general loss of clear insight; then you must confess that psychoanalysis has been right with both its assertions.

'Perhaps it was not entirely original in this. Many thinkers and students of mankind have said similar things, but our science has worked them out in detail and employed them to unravel many psychological riddles.'

We have here two propositions, two simple affirmations, whose consequences we have not finished evaluating: the first proposing that the unconscious of a healthy man harbours drives of hatred, murder and aggression; and the second proposing that intellect and reason are partly dependent on the emotions and the affective drives.

Starting from here, the issue is to strengthen man's tendencies to autonomy and co-operation, to prepare the conditions for the advent of a genuine democracy by liberating man from alienations, idolatries and fundamentalisms. But Freud has taught us that the rot always sets in; and indeed, Freud's work itself has fallen victim to idolators and fundamentalists. Moreover, the democratic project may itself be an illusion. Only the work of education can genuinely allow the development of autonomy, of self-confidence and of critical reflection. We know that this work is essential, that it must be constant even if it is possible that it will never be finished. As Freud said, we have at our disposal sources of energy out of all proportion to those which previous civilisations have known; yet when a constitution governed by its drives comes to exercise extraordinary powers over physical energy and biological processes, this is a recipe for a possible disaster for humanity. Our only chance of survival, he thought, is for critical reason to be cultivated *among all men*, and not for us to preserve the methods of intimidating thought which have been used, during thousands of years, to tame the individual.

So Freud had hope for the future of civilisation. He did not allow himself to think that we might never try to set up a valuable form of education, an education which he called 'irreligious'. Simultaneously pessimistic and full of hope, he wrote: 'perhaps there is a treasure to be dug up capable of enriching our

Threads which in the course of my development had become intertangled have now begun to separate; interests which I had acquired in the later part of my life have receded, while the older and original ones become prominent once more ... My interest, after making a lifelong détour through the natural sciences, medicine and psychotherapy, returned to the cultural problems which had fascinated me long before, when I was a youth scarcely old enough for thinking.

Postscript to An Autobiographical Study

civilization and ... it is worth making the experiment of an irreligious education. Should the experiment prove unsatisfactory, I am ready to give up all the reform and to return to my earlier, purely descriptive judgement that man is a creature of weak intelligence who is ruled by his instinctual wishes.'

This 'irreligious education' is in fact close to the 'religious' message of the great spiritual masters of humanity who hope for liberation from fear, hatred, illusion and idolatry. We must remember that when Freud spoke of religion, he meant any belief which rests on illusion and which keeps the human being in a state of childhood.

The real issue is to liberate mankind from internal war – the primary cause of external war – and from 'psychological misery', the source of other miseries, by allowing him to understand that it is not just outside him, but also inside him, ever-present, and that, while he certainly is partly the plaything of his determinisms, he is also free and responsible. But we need to understand 'that we were wrong to consider our intelligence as an independent force and not to take account of its subordination to the emotional life', and to have the courage to 'remain standing in our own obscurity.'

The big problem, as he often observed, is the psychological misery of the masses, and it is certainly necessary to see that the elites are included in those masses. The psychological misery which prevents man from maximising his potential for love and creativity, is both the result of civilisation and yet also the thing which risks destroying civilisation. 'As a result of this primary hostility which sets men up against one another, civilised society is constantly threatened with ruin. The interest of common work is not sufficient to maintain it: the instinctive passions are stronger than rational interests.'

Freud said clearly that our civilisation is in danger of death; like an individual, it may destroy itself by suicide or illness. Before Auschwitz and Hiroshima, Freud reminded Lou Andreas-Salomé in a letter that if we fail, there is nothing left for us but to withdraw, and the great unknown which destiny hides will resume cultural experiments of the same sort with a new race. We can understand this threat of destruction even more strongly today, because humanity has acquired terrifying weapons of destruction which can snuff out life on earth in an instant, like the flame of a candle. Fanaticisms have always accompanied the history of humanity, but today they have at their disposal the means to destroy us completely.

I repeat: Freud considered psychoanalysis as the *beginning* of a long quest. What he wanted was to 'disturb the sleep of the world', to be the denigrator of all illusions, whether religious or ideological, and of everything which hides under the appearance of idealism. The 'most beautiful of cathedrals' is still to be built, on the ruins of the illusions.

Freud died, despairing and disenchanted, chased out of Vienna by the forces of destruction which had once again appropriated the appearance of idealism, but as he said to one of his last correspondents: 'The spring is magnificent and so is love.'

And now, there is work to embark upon.

More than ever, it is essential that we take up again the project of which psychoanalysis represents a first attempt at elaboration and realisation. Didn't Freud himself take up the work begun by the philosophers of the Enlightenment? And this precisely because the

I have often said that I hold that the purely medical importance of analysis is outweighed by its importance to science as a whole, and that its general influence by means of clarification and the exposure of error exceeds its therapeutic value to the individual.

Letter to Pfister, 18th January 1928

central themes of the Enlightenment thought – the struggle against different forms of temporal or religious oppression – became topical again just at the moment when Freud was discovering psychoanalysis. With the rise of new forms of totalitarianism, and with the enormous increase in tribalism, new forms of tyranny – more violent and more massive – are appearing.

'As regards the therapeutic application of our knowledge,' he added, 'what would be the use of the most correct analysis of social neurosis, since no one possesses authority to impose such a therapy upon the group? But in spite of all these difficulties, we may expect that one day someone will venture to embark upon a pathology of cultural communities.'

As Stefan Zweig, Sigmund Freud's biographer, has written: 'He has made a magnificent beginning, and the gate stands open. Wherever the human spirit perceives beckoning distances and unexplored depths, it will not rest upon its old ways, but will move eagerly forward and unfold its indefatigable pinions.'

Select Bibliography

Sigmund Freud (Hogarth Press)
(1900a) *The Interpretation of Dreams*
(1910a [1909]) *Five Lectures on Psycho-Analysis*
(1916-17 [1915-17]) *Introductory Lectures on Psycho-Analysis*
(1917a) 'A Childhood Recollection from *Dichtung und Wahrheit*'
(1921c) *Group Psychology and the Analysis of the Ego*
(1926a) 'To Romain Rolland'
(1926e) *The Question of Lay Analysis*
(1927c) *The Future of an Illusion*
(1930a [1929]) *Civilization and its Discontents*
(1933a [1932]) *New Lectures on Psycho-Analysis*
(1933b [1932]) *Why War?*
(1935a) Postscript to *An Autobiographical Study*
(1960a) *Letters 1873-1939* (ed. E.L. Freud)
(1963a [1909-39] *Psycho-Analysis and Faith – the letters of Sigmund Freud and Oskar Pfister* (ed. H. Meng & E.L. Freud)

Ernest Jones
Sigmund Freud; Life and Work (Hogarth Press, 3 vols)

Michael Molnar (ed.)
Freud Diaries, 1929-39 (1992)

Marthe Robert
The Psychoanalytic Revolution (Allen & Unwin, 1966)

Stefan Zweig
Sigmund Freud – in *Mental Healers* (Cassell, 1933)